CURATIV

MENTAL HEALTH, HOPE, AND HEALING

WRITTEN BY

GINA CAPOBIANCO

COVER ART BY

SHANNON FELDMANN

Books by Gina Capobianco

Cognizant Introspection
Conscious Connection

In Loving Memory of

Carol A. Harrison
Mentor, Coach, and Friend

TABLE OF CONTENTS

BEHIND THE FAÇADE

TREADING WATER

EMERGING LIGHT

THE POWER OF WRITING

Acknowledgements

There are many people who have remained by my side on my journey. These people have been lights on the path. Mere words cannot express my gratitude. Thank you – Shannon Feldmann, Dr. Richard Klein, Carol Nichols, Pam Martin, and Sarah Usmani.

I would like to thank Shannon Feldmann for creating the cover for *Curative Quest: Mental Health, Hope, Healing*. Her paintbrush brings my poetry to life.

Thank you to my family.

A special thank you to Sheri Fink for providing professional guidance and encouragement.

I would like to thank Michelle Josette for editing and AJ Cosmo for page and cover layout.

FOREWORD

When we read poetry, something magical happens.

It doesn't matter what the intention of the poet is, it doesn't matter if you don't 'get it'. It doesn't matter if you don't know all the words or if you can't recognise the beat. It doesn't matter if you think the poem isn't aimed at you or if you're reading the poem in translation.

All that matters is that you see something, anything, however small, that chimes in with your own experience. Because when we connect to a poem, we see that we're not alone. The world is huge, with millions of people in it, but sometimes a poem, with a few words on a white page, can reach to our soul. This is especially true with poems about mental health because we see the suffering of others reflected in our own lives. Mental illness makes us feel isolated, ignored, and scared. You're convinced that it's just you whose feels and thinks the way you do. You feel like a stranger to yourself and to everybody else. Surely nobody else has those kinds of intrusive, alienating thoughts? Surely no one else goes to those dark strange places that I do? But we do, so many of us do, and we need to speak to each other. In *Stars in the Night Sky*, Gina writes:

> *"The world is too vast a place for it to be just me.*
> *If the stars connected could we find each other"*

There is an intimacy to poetry that makes us pull up our chair, grab a warming drink, and walk down the path alongside the poet. Poetry is perfect to express our mental health experiences because less words have more power. As the British writer Alan Bennett said, with poetry 'You can do more with less'. One carefully chosen word can mean more than pages and pages of text. Poetry gets to the crux of our feelings more quickly than anything else.

My own experiences with depression started as a child, although I didn't have a name to call the hellish low moods I experienced. As a teenager all I could describe it as was 'feeling ill'. "I feel as if something awful is going to happen," I would tell my mother. An impending doom. Depression then danced around with me most of my adult life but finally broke my toes a few days after my fortieth birthday. I collapsed completely, unable to look after myself and crucially for me, not able to read. But I could write, and writing allowed me some release.

In this collection of poems, Gina writes about her journey from darkness to slowly emerging light. At first we are caught in a wave of despair; depression and anxiety has taken over and it seems like there is no way out. Depression is strong and fierce and won't let go. Depression is making us feel alone and lost. It's crucial to include 'dark' poems in this collection because depression takes us over almost completely and we need to see that others experience that too. Even though there might be light ahead, it's impossible for us to see.

Then, change happens, as it always will, and brings an acceptance and some respite. Then the light starts to shine more brightly, light is hope. Hope is a precious, fallible commodity with depression, and it's hope that we need to survive. Sometimes the light comes and goes, sometimes it feels like it's gone forever, but although it's a flickering light, it's definitely there.

As Gina says in *Following a New Path*:

> "The path is bumpy.
> I stumble at times; lose my footing occasionally.
> Still I move forward; timid yet determined.
> I move toward the beckoning light."

The poetry in this collection is deeply personal. Gina describes her feelings, her everyday reactions to her world, and the ups and downs of her moods. But the words and messages are not so personal to exclude us. The poems are not cluttered with inaccessible metaphors and flowery language that you need a dictionary and a professor of literature onside to explain it to you. To my mind, the best poems, the most skilled writing, comes when the poet can distil their thoughts with words that the reader can understand. Those of us who are unwell need poems that we can pick up, easily relate to, and that reach out their hands to hold us. That is what this collection does.

James Withey
Brighton & Hove, UK, 2018
Founder of The Recovery Letters Project www.therecoveryletters.com
Editor of "The Recovery Letters: Addressed to People Experiencing Depression"

Introduction

We are all on our own journeys in life. These journeys can take us through dark times; times when we are not sure we can make it. I have known this darkness well. The darkness has overtaken my life at times, but it has also made me the person I am. I have grown through my experiences with the darkness of depression and anxiety. Curative Quest has emerged from my journey.

My perspective in this book is based on my experiences with depression and anxiety. However, other mental health disorders such as, but not limited to, schizophrenia, bipolar disorder, and obsessive-compulsive disorder can be viewed through a similar lens. Mental health disorders impact many people at different times in their lives. The impact varies from person to person. Whether the impact is mild or severe, the person deserves the best resources that can be offered. Mental health disorders are often paralyzing. They can make it difficult to get through even the simplest of life's tasks.

Some people try to hide the disorders. I tried to hide the depression and anxiety for a long time. It can be embarrassing to admit that I am depressed or anxious. I know I have a lot of positives in my life, but sometimes it is difficult to focus on those when the messages in my head are so dark. Depression and anxiety do not always make sense. Sometimes the messages they send contradict reality. On the outside everything appears to be going well, but on the inside I am struggling just to get through the day. I worry that other people will not understand what I am feeling and thinking. That is why it is often easier to try to hide a mental health disorder. Fortunately, I have learned that I cannot receive the support I need if I am hiding.

It is my belief that we need to give attention to mental health disorders. A stigma exists in society. People often do not want to talk about mental health, but this dialogue is crucial. We must do more as a society to ensure that mental health is discussed and that people affected by mental health disorders receive the support and care they need. Mental health needs to be a priority in today's society as it can impact every aspect of a person's life

It is important to acknowledge that oftentimes we need the assistance of others to climb out of the darkness. We have to reach out and accept the hands that are offered to us, whether those hands are from family, friends, or health care providers. Mental health disorders cannot be battled alone. We need the support of others. That support is going to look different for everyone, but it starts with understanding. The individual suffering from the mental health disorder needs to understand that he or she needs support. Other people need to understand that caring can make a difference. It might just be listening to someone. A phone call or text message is a small act to let a person know you are there and can bring light into the darkness a person feels. It might be taking a loved one's hand and guiding them to a social event. Other times it will be driving someone to a support group or therapy appointment. Whatever form it takes, being there for someone with a mental health disorder will not always be easy, but it can make a difference in a person's life.

THE HEALTH CARE CONNECTION

It is my belief that health care professionals, especially primary care providers, are the first line of defense for many individuals. Primary care providers can and should screen for mental health. However, it is more than just using a screening tool. They need to engage in conversations with their patients.

The patient needs to be more than just a medical chart. I have experienced different types of care from medical professionals. I have experienced the primary care provider who seemed preoccupied with moving on to the next patient. I have also been lucky enough to have been cared for by a provider who took the time to get to know me and listen to what I was saying, as well as what I was not saying. Both experiences provided me with learning opportunities that have led me to be a better advocate for my own health. From the first one, I learned it is important for me to speak up for myself. I must take an active role in my healing process. This is not always easy, but it is necessary. If a person cannot advocate for his or herself, it is critical that a loved one or friend step into this role.

The provider who listened taught me what I should expect from medical professionals. Now I understand that I deserve to be listened to when I see a doctor or other health care professional. The communication is a two-way street, but the medical professional must understand that he or she should open the door for the communication.

WRITING AS A HEALING TOOL

Writing has been an integral part of my ability to deal with depression and anxiety. For me writing usually takes the form of poetry, but I believe any form of writing can be healing. It is the act of providing an outlet for the feelings and emotions that are inside of a person. When I write I feel the release of feelings that are pent up inside of me. When those feelings are released I often feel better.

DARK POETRY

Many of us who suffer from mental health disorders grow accustomed to wearing masks. We hide behind a façade that says we are okay when inside we are crumbling. Many of the poems in the Behind the Façade and Treading Water sections represent what it can feel like when depression and anxiety take control.

Why include the dark poems in a book about mental health and healing? The depression and anxiety are real. They will not go away on their own. They have to be acknowledged and processed. While these poems are my experiences, I know that I am not alone in these feelings and thoughts. All over the world people struggle with mental health. It is important for individuals to know they are not alone. I share these poems to let others connect. It is my way of reaching out and saying, "I understand that feeling."

THE LIGHT OF HEALING

In my poetry, light often represents healing. The Emerging Light section contains poems reflecting on that healing. These poems offer hope. There are times when the darkness of depression and anxiety lifts and I can see light. The poems represent the part of my journey when I feel better about myself. This section is witness to the fact that even when a person suffers from depression and anxiety, there is reason for hope.

The Power of Writing section includes poems about how I have found healing in writing. These poems express the role writing has played in my journey and how poetry and writing have become an important part of my healing. I hope these poems might inspire someone else to pick up a pen.

THE ROLE OF POETRY IN MY LIFE

I have written poetry since I was a teenager. When I first started writing I did not understand why I was writing. Most of those early poems were filled with despair and hopelessness. Looking back I realize that the early poetry filled a role in my life. It was the therapy I was not receiving. I was letting out all of the depression that had consumed me. In a way I bled on the pages. That does not sound very healing, but it was. I learned to write poetry as a coping mechanism. It allowed me to release the negative emotions that had built up inside of me.

Today I am still writing poetry. Sometimes it is dark. Depression and anxiety come and go, but I have learned to cope with them. Other times it reflects the hope and healing I have experienced. The poetry still has the same curative effect. It allows me to release what I am feeling.

For years I was afraid to share my writing; embarrassed by its content. My poetry is very personal. The poems reflect how I felt at the time I wrote them. They are the "me" hiding behind the façade I show the world. I was afraid that people would not understand my struggles. Once I started sharing I realized there are people who understand and just as importantly, others who want to understand. Sharing my poetry has provided me with more healing. In sharing my poetry and speaking about it, I have brought more light into my journey.

I eventually came to the realization that I wanted to share my journey. Incredible "lights" have guided me as I have struggled with depression and anxiety. Maybe by sharing my poetry and my story I can be a light for someone else.

My journey is not over. I still have periods of darkness when the depression and anxiety take over. The difference is I now have hope. Healing is a reality. I know I will always deal with mental health issues. It is a part of who I am, but it does not define me. I can overcome the dark times.

BEHIND THE FAÇADE

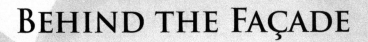

DEPRESSION

Depression hurts.
It is a silent pain,
Often hidden from others.
A smile on the outside masks the torment within my mind.
Words spin in my head.
Thoughts that will not stop create a barrage that drags me down.
No one hears these thoughts.
Others cannot comprehend the pain caused by these nagging words.
Depression is a lonely condition,
One that so often a person battles alone.
Out of fear that others will not understand, I isolate myself.
The depression gathers strength.
I worry others will notice and think I am weak.
Despite knowing the depression is real,
I fear others will belittle my affliction.
Society does not recognize the reality of depression.
People tell me to cheer up.
They do not understand that I would if I could.
There is no on and off switch.
I will continue to fight the depression.
Some days the depression will win,
Other days I will win.
A lifelong battle with an invisible illness.
Depression hurts, depression debilitates,
But my silent battle perseveres.

ANXIETY RISING

I feel the anxiety rise in my chest,
An uneasy feeling that I cannot explain.
My thoughts start to swirl.
With closed eyes I tell myself to relax,
But the anxiety tightens its grip upon me.
My mind begins to race,
Thoughts no longer content to just swirl.
I feel the tension spread through my body.
The anxiety will not let go. It builds.
I am trapped within its grasp.
My appearance shows no clues to the anxiety mounting within me,
But inside I am losing control.
The rising anxiety becomes physical pain.
I search for an escape I know I will not find.
The anxiety controls me,
Buries me in its consuming snare.

MY WALLS

The world around me spins with daily commotion.
I feel out of place.
Like I am standing still amongst the whir of activity.
The bustle confuses me as I long to be a part,
But do not know how to enter that world.
I remain isolated on the periphery;
Staring at all that goes on around me.
Until finally I retreat behind my own walls.
Secure, free from the dizziness that attracts, yet frightens me.
My walls extend their reach to further separate me from the world.
Often I stare at the walls content in knowing I am not a part of the other side.
Other times I shed tears as I wish to be a part of something that can never be.
My walls shake, remind me that so much goes on without me.
Despite the shaking I remain secure behind my walls.

Fettered

Fettered by anxiety, I struggle to find piece of mind.
It is a daily fight.
Some days I lack the strength to engage in the battle.
I hide from the world, afraid to let my weaknesses show.
The vise that strangles me tightens its grip.
Falling to the ground, I cry out,
But it is a silent cry.
No one can hear me.
My anxiety rises.
I cannot continue the battle.
Anxiety has won.

THE GRIP OF DEPRESSION

The depression has overtaken my life once again.
I am paralyzed.
Lying here with no ambition,
As always I am alone.
No one to talk to, no one to interact with.
I have isolated myself.
It hurts so much, but I cannot make it go away.
So I lie here wishing the depression would ease its grip upon me.
Praying the phone will ring and someone will be on the other end.
There is no ring.
No one searches for me.
No one reaches out.
Depression has cast its net upon me;
Tightened its hold.
I cannot free myself.
I am trapped;
Forever held within the grip of depression.

STORM SURGE

Storm surge.
An emotional buildup.
A giant swell shakes my whole body.
Anxiety cracks like lightning within my mind.
I am shaking.
The raw, intense emotions flood through me.

Storm surge.
An avalanche of thoughts.
The building noise is deafening.
Depression bears down upon me.
I am crying.
An ebony darkness penetrates my entire being.

Storm surge.
A searing heat.
The roaring clap of thunder reverberates through me.
Physical pain consumes me.
I am falling.
The damp earth breaks my landing.

Storm surge.
An ominous silence.
The stillness of the air thickens.
Suffocation grips me.
I am gasping.
An emptiness absorbs me.

Storm surge.
Tossed upon the sandy beach,
My emotions lie peacefully
As the mind storm has blown back out to sea.

Interior, Exterior

On the exterior my life seems fine.
I portray a woman who belongs,
But on the inside I struggle to fit in.
The smile on my face hides the pain I feel.
While others believe this façade is really me, I know the truth.
Within my mind I am a mess.
Thoughts wreak havoc.
The emotional toll is more than I can bear.
I cannot continue to maintain this exterior when my interior is falling apart.
Slowly I step away and
Extract myself from the world.

EXISTENCE

A disposable existence,
My existence.
Stumbling through life in a haze.
Purposeless, lifeless.
Tossed to the periphery.
Isolated, abandoned.
Tears burn, my heart aches.
Silence, deafening silence.
Disregarded like a piece of trash.
Useless, worthless.
My disposable existence.

THE DARK ABYSS

Depression overruns my thoughts, leaving me unable to cope with day-to-day occurrences.
The battle rages within my mind.
Darkness grips my thoughts tightly.
I am inundated by an urge to give in, to let everything fall to pieces.
I spend my life in denial,
Pretending that I do not feel the pain.
Behind a fake smile lies the darkness that abounds within me.
I struggle, but am unable to overcome depression's grip.
Like a searing fire it leaves me charred.
Memories of better times turned to ash.
Consumed with self-denigration, I have lost all self-worth.
Depression has destroyed my hope;
Left me alone in the dark abyss that is my life.

Life's Reflection

The pain of my life's reflection is more than I can bear.
Some say to just let it all go.
Others say I have more happiness than I think,
But I know I am not where I wanted to be at this point in my life.
The pictures my younger self painted in my mind were very different than what I have experienced.
The canvas of my life is now filled with dark colors.
Gray clouds have replaced the rainbows of my youthful hope.
Rain drops fall.
My vision blurs as I wipe away my tears.
I realize tomorrow will be no different than today.

BROKEN

I am hurting.
I cannot look at myself.
Self-loathing fills me.
Sometimes I do not want to live.
There does not seem to be a purpose to my life.
I have wasted so much.
I am worthless.
Each day haunts me.
I wish I could erase the pain;
Forget the dread that washes over me.
Life holds no meaning for me, only emptiness.
My life is a void.
I am alone.
Interactions destroy me.
Leave me battered.
I inflicted the bruises upon myself.
Struggle to lift my head as I hope no one sees me.
I want to exit this world and leave behind the pain.
I have no strength remaining.
Broken, I take leave of life.

MY OWN ISOLATION

I am alone in this world.
Each day I battle loneliness.
Tell myself tomorrow will be different,
But I know I am just kidding myself.
I will always be alone.
I have nothing to offer anyone.
No one wants to spend time with me.
I have no reason to believe that will ever change.
Sometimes I wonder if I even want it to change.
I make little attempt to improve my social situation.
There is no one to blame except myself.
Loneliness consumes me;
Depresses me as I continue to isolate myself.
I create my own misery.
Wallow in the loneliness that is my reality.

THE VOID

I realize there is something missing in my life;
A void that tears me apart.
Emptiness envelops me,
Leaves me aching.
Each day brings more of the same;
Raw loneliness, isolation.
I fear a continuation of these emotions, but I have become complacent.
Accepting my loneliness, I step back when I should step forward.
I allow the isolation to consume me as my life continues to pass me by.
I stand in the shadows waiting for invitations that will never come.
Darkness settles around me, clings to me.
I no longer search for the light.
Instead I crawl within myself, content yet broken.
Doubt builds up.
Healing is out of reach.
I close my eyes and
Accept the void that is my life.

TEARS

Tears fill my eyes as once again I question my worth.
I am fading,
Ready to run and hide from the world.
I do not know how many more downfalls I can bear.
The tears blind me, leave a stinging sensation in my eyes.
I have nothing to offer.
I am useless.
So much of my life wasted.
Tears flow down my face.
The floodgates have opened.
I drop to my knees;
Say a silent prayer that will go unanswered.
The value of my life is little.
I amount to nothing.
Tears are all I have.

REAL PAIN

Ubiquitous fears haunt me.
Self-doubt reigns over me.
Each day I struggle to make peace with myself.
Companionship eludes me.
Darkness clouds my vision.
I am alone,
Afraid to ask the questions that must be asked.
Each day I sink a little lower.
Depression settles upon me.
My spirit withers as I lose hope.
I close my eyes; wonder if it is all a dream,
But the pain is too real.

Falling Into the Abyss

The abyss of darkness is once again open.
I feel myself falling.
My body spinning as I spiral down.
Darkness has returned, taken hold of my thoughts.
Pulling me deeper and deeper into the isolation that overcomes me.
I cannot control this free fall.
I have lost hope; lost my will to continue the battle.
I raise my hands in surrender;
Close my eyes.
The abyss has swallowed me.

THE NOISE

Commotion fills my mind.
I want to run away.
My efforts have been wasted.
All I hear is noise.
My brain feels as if it is about to explode.
I have nothing left to give.
No strength to continue.
I fear that I will crack into pieces before I can get away.
So much noise pounding in my head.
I crave silence;
Search for a refuge,
But I am floundering.
Like a fish out of water I am no longer in my element.
I run from the noise, but cannot hide.
My demise is forthcoming.
I will welcome the silence it will bring
As I lower my head and wait.

THE SHADES OF LONELINESS

Loneliness comes in different shades.
Some shades more painful than others.
All leave a sting.
The darker the shade of loneliness, the greater the sense of isolation.
I have experienced many shades in my lifetime.
Loneliness in the presence of others is by far the worst.
I have encountered this darkest of shades so often.
It is a pain that cannot be adequately explained in mere words.
One must experience its cruelty,
Breathe in its shadow to understand.
Stand next to someone who does not see you, someone who ignores
your presence.
Lack of interaction has left me forever scarred.
The shades of loneliness have consumed me.

THE ONSLAUGHT

A tumultuous onslaught of thoughts overwhelms me.
The noise is more than I can bear.
I try to silence the uproar, but it just reverberates throughout my mind.
My attempts are futile.
The deafening echo of negativity drags me down.
I fear that I will never experience the calm of inner silence.
My thoughts are jumbled within this cacophony.
I am unable to summon the strength to quiet these thoughts.
I long for silence,
But the onslaught consumes me.
In constant battle with my ruminations, my spirit is broken;
My will to continue sapped by the persistent chatter.

AN EMPTY STARE

I am in tears again.
It is too much for me to bear.
My life is not what I wanted.
I am not sure what I really want from life.
All I know is that I cannot go on this way.
I do not like what I see in the mirror.
My pain is reflected back at me.
It stares at me; mocks me.
I cry as I look into the wicked glass.
I hate my own reflection; detest its empty stare.
Warm tears stream down my face.
I shiver with the realization that I am forever trapped in an existence I cannot endure.

LONELY STAGNATION

Lonely stagnation.
My life.
Alone each night,
Shunned by human contact.
Embraced by nothingness.
Lonely stagnation.
Night after night,
Faceless, I glance at myself in a mirror.
Wonder who I have become,
Question if I ever really was anybody.
Darkness fades,
Light emerges.
I don my mask and face the world.
My days are a charade hiding my faceless existence.
I engage with others until the darkness returns.
I exit the daytime world,
Remove my mask.
Lonely stagnation.
Its familiarity breeds my contempt.
I sink into the depths of isolation.
The evening—an unwelcomed reprieve from interaction.

When the Words Win

The stress of my mind's endless negative chatter reduces me to tears.
I cry as the voices within my head announce my worthlessness for the countless time.
My strength is sapped.
The relentless voices echo in my head, tear me down.
For so long I have tried to overcome this chatter,
But I no longer have the will to fight.
I close my eyes,
Feel the warm tears as they fall down my cheeks.
A sense of déjà vu reminds me that I have been here before.
Yet despite this familiarity I cannot seem to overcome the pain.
The voices are no longer content to merely chatter.
They begin to shout.
I am overwhelmed.
I cannot quiet the noise.
Behind my tears I cower, raise my hands to cover my ears.
It is no use.
The noise is within my mind.
The shouts grow louder.
I fall to the ground
As the voices pierce through my mind.
I feel myself give in.
My strength is completely gone.
I have nothing left.
The voices have won.

COWARD

Jagged corners and sharp edges keep me trapped.
I dare not risk torn flesh.
Coward!
Where is my strength?
I have remained hidden for so long;
Cowering in the shadows, afraid to step forward.
No room to step backward.
Years of hiding have left me empty, alone.
Jagged corners and sharp edges protect me.
Behind the rigid walls they create, I am safe.
No harm can come to me.
Coward!
Why am I afraid to live?

JUST AS A FLOWER WILTS

Flowers wilting in the sun remind me just how fragile life can be.
Brown-tinged petals fall to the ground.
A bee flies away.
Gray clouds fill the sky.
I walk through the dying garden.
A sense of connection overcomes me.
I see myself in the limp flowers,
Understand why they have turned away from the sun.
I, too, am wilting.
No longer feel the sun's warmth.
My head bows to the ground as my life withers away.

Enduring Pain

False hope derails my journey.
For a time I thought I saw the light.
Perhaps it was just a mirage or the glow of some distant happiness.
Whatever it is, it was not meant for me.
How foolish I have been to allow my hopes to be raised.
Hope only brings pain,
Extinguishes the light.
Even a flicker is too much to ask for.
My world is meant to be dark.
Darkness suits me.
I give up.
No reason to smile remains.
Wishful thinking, hopes, and dreams serve only to destroy.
For me there is no hope,
Only the enduring pain of darkness.

I WAS WRONG

Maybe I misjudged,
Anticipated something that is not to be.
It has happened before.
My mistake would be nothing new.
I get ahead of myself and forget my reality for a moment,
But reality is never far away.
At times it slaps me in the face;
Reminds me of all that I lack.
With tear-filled eyes and a numb heart I remember.
Never again will I let down my guard.
I have built walls around myself for a reason.
It is foolish to let them down.
I allowed myself to be fooled, to believe there might be more to life.
I could not have been more wrong.
It is time for me to retreat behind the walls I had built.
Hide from the world.
There is nothing left for me.

NEVER MIND

I reached out to you,
But you were not there.
Never mind.
I do not need you.
There is no one here for me.
Nothing left for me to be a part of.
At one time I convinced myself that you cared;
Believed the lies I told myself.
I was going to share with you.
Let you be a part of my life,
But you showed no interest.
Never mind.
I forgot that you do not care.

FAMILIAL PAIN

Why is family able to hurt one another so much?
I feel out of place.
I do not belong.
Like trying to insert a square peg into a round hole,
I do not fit.
You ignore me; treat me as if I am invisible.
Perhaps I am.
So often I wish I could disappear.
Maybe then the pain would not feel so real.
I look at you and wonder what I did.
We are family, but there is no love for me.
The hope that once filled my heart dissipates with each wound inflicted by my growing isolation.
I realize that I am alone.
Life holds no joy for me as I have no one to share it with.
I no longer hold on to the hope of familial love.
I am forever alone.

ANOTHER HOLIDAY

Another holiday spent alone.
Just a day like any other.
I am by myself, isolated from others.
No family, no friends; just me sitting with this journal.
Words on paper become my companions.
Words echo from deep within my consciousness.
I am acutely aware of my isolation;
Fear it though I have embraced its familiarity.
A holiday is just another lonely day.
No reason to celebrate.
No need for companionship.
I have become accustomed to my aloneness;
Stare at walls with wonder;
Write with ease as my emotions pour forth.
Holidays are just ordinary squares on the calendar of my isolated life.

TIME TO DISAPPEAR

I have made so many attempts,
Put forth too much effort.
The time has come for me to accept the reality I already know to be
true.
I am worthless to you.
I always have been.
Now I am ready to give in and accept that I should disappear.
You will never notice me.
I have feelings, but you do not care.
I am nothing to you.
I will disappear.
Never bother you again.

Rude Awakening

A rather rude awakening greets me;
Leaves me stunned.
I feel as if I have been slapped in the face.
The sting breaks my will.
I give up.
I tried so hard;
Thought I had done everything right.
I could not have been more wrong.
Betrayed; laughed at from behind closed doors.
What a fool I have been!
Left with no options, I prepare to leave this all behind.

TREADING WATER

SINKING

I realize I am not okay.
I struggle to keep myself afloat.
I am drowning.
Life pulls me under.
I try to keep my head up, but I am sinking.
I feel my mind go limp before my body does.
My arm reaches up, but there is nothing to grab on to.
I see only darkness though my eyes are open.
The downward pull is too much.
I am ready to give in.
Sinking deeper, I am submerged.
I struggle to breathe as I feel the fight being pulled out of me.
My strength is gone.
No longer floating, I sink into nothingness.

OUR TRUE SELF

Within us lies a self that others rarely see.
It is our true self, hidden deep within.
Lying underneath all the lies society has told us;
Beneath the scars damp with tears.
This true self is who we really are.
The person we were meant to be.
Yet it remains hidden, forced into the recesses of our being.
When we were very young it did not hide.
As small children we were free to be ourselves
Until our innocence became lost.
Quickly we learned that our true self was not good enough.
Others told us so.
So we learned to hide.
At first it was a game of pretend.
Our true self snuck out at times.
As we grew older our true self had to hide more often.
Soon we did not recognize ourselves.
A masquerade had begun.
Yet our true self remained hidden, forced into the recesses of our being.
We continued to age and still we played hide and seek.
No one knew who we truly were.
No one really cared.
We conformed to society's ideal;
Our true self hidden from others.
This game wears on us, tears at our soul.
So we bury our true self a little deeper.
Keep it hidden from the world.
Robbing the world of the gifts we truly bear.
Imprisoned deep within us a rumble begins.
A slow beating at first;
A pang gaining momentum.
As our true self, first hidden as a child, longs to emerge.
We struggle; try to ignore the call.
The noise becomes deafening.
Others begin to notice.
"What is wrong with you?" they ask.
Our true self fights to be heard.
But we silence it.
Look them in the eyes and say,
"Nothing. I am fine."
Force our true self back down and
Continue this charade called life.

MY CHARADE

A new year, but the same old me,
Struggling to be whole.
I fight against all that drags me down.
My strength is waning.
Darkness consumes my thoughts,
Haunts my dreams.
I am left crying.
Unsure I can keep up this charade,
Each day I go through the motions.
Pretend that I am okay when just under the surface I am breaking
down.
Pieces of my life tinged with hopelessness.
I am falling apart.
Sadly, I am not even sure I want to be put back together.
Nonetheless, my tears continue to fall.
I go through the motions
As my charade continues.

Awake Once Again

Once again I cannot sleep.
The hour is late. The sky is dark.
Yet I lie awake wondering if sleep will ever come.
So often this is my night.
I am restless.
I long for the sweet slumber that eludes me.
Staring out the window, I see pitch darkness.
The moon provides a sliver of light.
Soon the sun will rise, replace the moon with its bright, orange hues.
Another night shall be wasted.
The day will be long.
I will wonder how I can get through it;
Only to lie awake once again tomorrow night.

Another Night

Each night is the same.
I struggle to find the sleep I so desperately need.
I close my eyes;
Hope sleep will find me tonight.
Minutes creep into hours and still I lie awake.
Another sleepless night.
Moonlight gives way to the rising sun and I finally drift into a night-
mare-filled slumber.
I awaken sweaty and unrested.
Another night has passed.

WITHOUT SLEEP

Awake again.
Dark skies outside my window.
The clock ticking past midnight.
My mind misunderstands; thinks it is time to wander.
Sleep hides.
I lie awake wondering when sleep will arrive.
Bring with it the refueling my body needs.
But sleep remains elusive.
The nightly wanderings of my mind leave me drained, mentally and
physically.
I have tried to relax my mind,
But each attempt has been in vain.
No remedy brings sleep.
Each night I find myself
Awake again.

I Cannot Understand Myself

No one else can understand what I do not understand myself.
My thoughts shrivel around one thought.
I cannot let go, though I desperately need to.
Still I cling to this one thought.
It tears me down, leaves me crying.
I must keep these emotions to myself.
No one can comfort me.
Alone, as always, I continue to battle my feelings.
I know there is nothing I can change.
No way to bring a smile to my face.

A Friend

I could use a friend today.
Someone to talk with, someone to share a smile.
So much of my time is spent alone.
I feel isolated and lost.
A friend would help me find my way;
Let me know that someone cared about me even when I do not care
too much about myself.

I could use a friend today.
Someone who knows what I am thinking even when I do not say the
words.
I could be a friend, too.
Listen and empathize.
Friendship would lift the loneliness,
Provide a reason for living.
I could use a friend today.

FOUR EMPTY WALLS

I lack the motivation to make the changes I need to make.
Despite knowing I cannot continue living this way,
I make no real efforts to change.
I stare at the walls and wonder why I am the way I am.
Fear isolates me, anxiety paralyzes me.
I remain alone even though I know the isolation is destroying me.
Past efforts to reach out have failed, leaving me afraid to try again.
So I sit here alone, four empty walls staring back at me.
My motivation sapped, I struggle to find a reason to connect with others.
I remain unchanged, a lost soul traveling the journey of life alone.

AN APPOINTMENT

Standing at a distance in your white lab coat, you barely listen.
You seem to ignore my words.
I wonder how you can help me when you are not listening.
It is obvious that you do not care.
Mechanically your stethoscope presses against me,
But I doubt you realize my heart is beating.
I am wasting your time.
You ask a question as you stare at your computer screen.
Despite the pains I feel, I cannot speak.
You are supposed to help me,
But you look right through me.
Your eagerness to be rid of me is written upon your face.
I feel the urge to leave the exam room;
Forget what I came for.
Leave without the care you should have provided.

UNCONTROLLED THOUGHTS

My mind wanders.
I have grown accustomed to its traveling.
Eventually my thoughts will come full-circle and
I will be back where I am in this present moment.
Until then I allow the thoughts to traverse as they must.
I cannot control my mind's thoughts.
For so long I tried, only to realize that I am not in control.
The thoughts overpower me.
Prevent me from seeing clearly.
Now I let go and take the ride.
Thoughts circle through my mind.
I remain in place,
Conditioned by thoughts I cannot control.

TEARS BEHIND YOUR EYES

I see the tears behind your eyes.
You are hurting though you try to hide the pain.
I reach out to you, but I do not know what to say.
There is so much that I wish I could do for you,
But I realize I do not know how.
For now all I can do is let you know that I am here.
I wish I knew how to help you.
I wish I carried the salve to heal your wounds.

Tomorrow's Promises

Vanishing into tomorrow's promises
I relinquish control of today.
Give away my power at a time when I should not let it go.
I cannot say I was not warned.
It is my fault.
I let my guard down.
Gave into false hope.
Now I am left lost and alone
With no one to blame except myself.

Strangers

No words uttered.
Are we even in the same space?
An invisible void lies between us.
I do not know you.
You do not know me.
We are merely two strangers immersed in our own worlds.
No reason exists for us to communicate.
Though we are connected, we live very separate lives.
The bond that should bring us together was broken long ago.
We have become strangers in each other's lives.
Words cannot heal if they are never spoken.
Silence permeates the fractured relationship
And we continue our lives as strangers.

WAITING

Waiting, waiting.
I am on edge.
Fear pulsates through my body, grips my mind.
The unknown holds me in a vise;
Consumes my thoughts.
I should reach out, attempt to find the answer on my own,
But I am afraid.
I tell myself that the answer cannot hurt me if I do not know wha
it is.
Foolish! I am foolish!
I must assert myself.
Stand up for me; take care of myself.
My hand reaches for the phone; begins to dial,
But my fingers freeze after two digits.
I am scared.
Waiting, waiting.
I cannot take much more.

Always Waiting

I wish I could walk away from the depression.
Say goodbye to the anxiety that consumes me.
For many years I have tried.
Ups and downs, good days and bad.
Though I long to give in, still I rise each morning to face the new day.
Aware of my struggles, I desire to forget them;
Place past pains behind me;
Leave the darkness.
With the rising sun I awaken into the light.
Pray the darkness never returns.
I distract myself, but the depression and anxiety are always waiting,
Filling me with a sense of trepidation for the future.
I find myself wondering if I will always be like this.
Ask if the depression will ever lift,
But no one answers my question.

YEARS FADE

Reflecting on my life, I wonder where time has gone.

So much I meant to do is still undone.

Days melt into each other.

Years fade without much change.

I have rarely noticed the calendar changing.

Now I am middle-aged and wonder what I have missed in life.

I sit here each night, alone except for the pen I write with and the music playing in the background.

Not much to reflect on.

I doubt the future will be much different.

Letting go of hope, I sit here and continue to reflect on what my life could have been.

Unanswered Questions

Why am I not good enough?
You did not even give me a chance.
Do I not deserve even the slightest bit of consideration?
I would settle for just your acknowledgement.
That is not going to happen, though, is it?
I give up.
I have lost my confidence.
Why did I even try?
Deep down I knew better.
The fault is all mine.
As much as I wish you would explain to me why I was pushed aside,
I know you will not.
Pain gnaws at me as I struggle to understand why you remained
silent.
Despite the pain, I do not blame you.
There must be a reason you have ignored me.
Maybe someday you will tell me what I did wrong;
Let me know what I am lacking.
Until then I will remain quiet.
I will lock my questions inside of me.
Trust that you have good reasons for allowing me to feel this way.
Perhaps I never should have tried;
Never opened that door.
Unfortunately, I cannot undo my actions.
I cannot turn back time and make a different decision.
I unfairly expected too much from you.
My intent was to better myself, but instead I have allowed my con-
fidence to be shattered.
I am done taking risks.
I give up.

UNKNOWN

You did not respond.
I do not understand.
Part of me wants to ask you why.
Another part of me fears the answer.
I will not ask you.
As much as I need to know,
Not knowing is somehow less painful.
I wonder if I can be content with not knowing.
I do not really have a choice.
My fear, my awkwardness, will not allow me to ask you.
The answer will remain unknown,
But I will always wonder.

A Friendship Unrequited

Sometimes I start wondering why I have put forth so much effort
toward a hopeless cause.
Friendship unrequited hurts as much as an ignored love of the heart.
I must move forward, honestly look at what is staring me in the face.
The relationship is not what I want it to be,
Nor will it ever be.
Friendship requires two people,
Not just the desire of one.
So with the pain of my jilted attempt I step away.
What I had hoped for can never become reality.
I must accept what I have now and
Allow myself to be denied this other desire.
A friendship unrequited, a chance whose time has passed.

CHASING DREAMS

Chasing dreams down a well-worn path,
I lost my way.
Light faded, clouds rolled in.
Soon all around me was dark.
I could not see what lay ahead of me.
My past obscured by the darkness behind me.
With halting steps I attempted to continue,
But my efforts were futile.
I stumbled upon raised hopes.
Emotionally bruised, I could not stand.
Tears blurred my vision.
A sharp pain penetrated my chest.
As I began to crawl, a voice called out to me;
Echoed in my ears.
I listened, but could not understand.
Nonsense was all I heard.
Reaching out I tried to find the voice, but there was nothing.
Silence erupted.
My dreams shattered around me.
Jagged pieces fell to the ground.
I picked up a random piece.
Felt its warmth dissipating.
A chill ran through me.
As the ground shook, the path I had been following cracked.
I opened my eyes.
No dreams were left to chase.

MEMORIES AND DREAMS

Vague memories,
Recurring dreams.
Sleepless nights spent tossing and turning leave me drained.
No energy to find the joy in life.
The memories haunt me; interrupt my thoughts.
Dreams disturb the little sleep my mind allows.
Still I enter each new day hopeful.
Until the anxiety builds and the depression drags me down.
I stumble through the day only to find I am trapped within the cycle.
Exhausted, I fall into bed at the end of the day.
Vague memories,
Recurring dreams emerge once again.
My slumber interrupted.
The hours dedicated to mind and body renewal are disturbed.
Night and day my life follows this pattern, a pattern created by disruption.

THE HAZE

Stumbling through life in a haze,
I walk into brick walls, crash into roadblocks.
With each step I become more hesitant,
Afraid of what lies ahead of me.
The past has traumatized me.
My world is a dark and desolate place.
Fear guides my steps, halts my pace.
I continue to stumble, trip over the barricades I have erected to pro-
tect myself.
The haze grows thicker, blinding me.
Still I stumble forward.
Fall and get back up again.
The haze thickens.
I can no longer see what lies ahead of me.
As the haze continues to thicken I lose my will to endure life.
I isolate myself from the world around me.
Close my eyes and become numb.
No longer attempting to move forward,
I stumble no more.

UNFINISHED DREAMS

Ephemeral slumber leaves me chasing illusory dreams.
The night sky has long since settled upon the evening,
My eyes are open; my body twists and turns in search of comfort.
I drift off into a fitful sleep.
Startled, I am awake once again.
Darkness fills the room, yet I feel as if it is mid-day.
Dreams have forsaken me, leaving me to imagine their ending.
The hours tick by, as I lie awake.
I wonder where the dreams would have taken me;
Wonder if I would have found inspiration.
As sleep eludes me, I can only contemplate unfinished dreams.
Ephemeral slumber curtails my dreams each night.

Depression's Paradox

Depression, a paradox in every sense of the word.
Everything to live for, yet a struggle to get through the day.
Sadness when laughter abounds.
Loneliness in a crowd.
Rain clouds filling a sunny sky,
The pain of not knowing the source of tears.
The paradox continues day and night.
Leaving confusion and hopelessness in its wake.
The depression lifts only to darken life once again.
A continuous cycle that must be lived to be understood.
There are good days and bad days.
The depression's control lies in the unknown.
Whether I will be energetic or lie in bed all day,
Smile with others or hide in tears.
I never know which me will emerge.
Depression, a paradox dominating my life.

I AM FOOLISH

I wish you knew the power that you hold over me.
If only I could tell you how much you are hurting me;
Somehow let you know that I am crying on the inside.
I admire you, respect you, but it does not matter.
I doubt you even notice me.
I am not really here.
It is okay.
I give up.
Worthless, that is what I am.
You have let me know what you think without saying a word.
I never should have taken the risk.
I belong holed up inside of myself.
No one can hurt me if I refuse to let anyone in.
I let you in and now what do I have?
Nothing.
The same nothingness that has encompassed my life.
It is not your fault.
I have brought on all of my own failings.
I create my own misery.
For a while I believed you cared, thought you were my friend.
Foolish! So foolish of me.
Maybe you did care at one time.
It does not matter now.
I will retreat inside of myself.
Create a place where I am safe.
I do not need you or anyone else.
My life is my life even with all of its failings.

RUN AWAY

I would like to run away.
Leave all of this pain behind.
Numbness awaits me;
A dulling of my senses so that I no longer feel the pain of isolation.
There is no place for me here.
I have never belonged.
I now know that I never will.
Slowly I rise to my feet,
Take the first steps toward the door.
Without glancing behind me I step through the door.
There is nothing behind me to look back upon.
Only memories of being ignored and forgotten.
I will not turn back.
With a quickening pace I move forward.
Where I am headed I have no way of knowing,
But anywhere has to be better.
I lift my head and run forward.

STARS IN THE NIGHT SKY

I sit and gaze at the stars overhead
Wondering if others feel the loneliness that has become so familiar
to me.
Someone else must be staring at the same stars
Filled with the same numbing emotion.
The world is too vast a place for it to be just me.
If the stars connected could we find each other;
Turn loneliness into camaraderie?
Lost souls staring at stars in the night sky.
Perhaps a world apart, yet connected by distant stars.

A PARADOXICAL REALITY

The light fades.
The silence becomes deafening.
A paradoxical reality.
Perhaps the joke is on me.
Maybe the truth is staring at me.
I have no idea where I am,
No knowledge of where I am going.
A heated debate within my mind stirs me, causes me to rise.
Yet the more I climb, the lower I sink.
The deeper I dig, the farther I have left to ascend.
Obscurity provides clarity.
Darkness fills my vision.
I fall to the ground and reach for the heavens.

Emerging Light

TRAVELING

Gazing at the night sky I see darkness.
Distant stars remind me the light is still there.
The darkness lasts only for a time.
Then gives way to the light of a new day.
With each sunrise, obstacles become faceable challenges.
Daylight brings new hope.
After a time the darkness will return to blot out the light.
As the days and nights chase each other I have learned their pattern.
Light and dark follow each other, taking me on a journey.
I experience ups and downs,
Traveling at a pace uniquely my own.
Night and day,
My journey continues from darkness into light.

LIFE'S JOURNEY

I follow the twists and turns on this road that is my life's journey.
It is leading me somewhere, but I do not know the destination.
I am not sure I even want to know.
The journey has been difficult.
At times I feel the warmth of the light,
See the world with clarity.
As I continue forward a haze creeps in,
Blurring my vision.
I am left unsure of myself, anxious and depressed.
Darkness settles upon me for the countless time.
Without the light I am lost.
The journey becomes daunting.
I cower in fear; isolate myself from others.
Life's journey drags me along.
Some days I want to give in;
Step off the trail into nothingness,
But I remain on the twisting journey.
I take small steps forward;
Continue living.
Daring life's twists and turns.
As I navigate this journey I remind myself that I have traveled many
similar roads.
I can find my way;
Arrive at my next destination ready to live.

FOLLOWING A NEW PATH

From the depths of my emotion I attempt to rise.
Strive to shed the darkness surrounding me.
I climb one hesitant step at a time.
Lift my head; open my eyes.
In the distance a light shines; beckons me.
I feel its warmth envelop me; welcome its soothing touch.
My steps quicken; become less tentative.
Gaining confidence I begin to believe I can find my way.
The light shines brighter as I near.
Hope radiates from within me.
A path I have never seen emerges in front of me.
I decide to follow this path; discover where it leads.
It is a risk I would not have taken in the past,
But I must take now.
I am ready for a change; prepared for the challenge.
Placing my right foot in front of my left, left in front of right, I embark on the journey.
The path is bumpy.
I stumble at times; lose my footing occasionally.
Still I move forward; timid yet determined.
I move toward the beckoning light.
Filled with hope, my steps become more confident.
Shadows disappear behind me.
The challenge has brought me close to the light.
I feel the healing beginning already.
Even though there are still bumps along the path, I know that I will make it.

The Power of Music

The music transports me into another realm;
Ushers me out of my depression if only for a short time.
Lyrics replace the thoughts that normally spin through my mind.
Guitar riffs and the mingling of ivory keys soothe me.
The bass and the drums beat through me.
My body moves with the rhythm.
I feel a peace only the music can provide.
As the music infuses the air I feel myself floating with it;
Watch my worries drift away.
Anxious thoughts slowly ease.
A smile supplants the depression.
The music fills me, allowing me to escape into a safe world.

Music Heals

Symphonic voices fill the air.
I gently sway to the music.
A sense of calm washes over me.
Peace enters my mind as the lyrics replace the noise.
Rhythmic beating, energizing riffs soothe me.
The anxiety within me abates.
I become one with the music;
Lose myself as the song takes over.
The chorus repeats.
I listen to its message and understand.
My body relaxes as the tension leaves me.
The music frees me, allows me to heal.

GRACE

A soulful voice serenades me as I contemplate life.
Raw emotion overpowers my pain.
The voice soothes me; settles my anxiety.
Lyrics written as if intended for me.
I feel the energy; engage in healing.
Songs speaking directly to me.
When I am about to break, I turn to the voice.
It lifts me from the brink as it always has.
The voice has taught me to "Let It Go" and hold on to life.
I close my eyes; allow the voice to carry me into the lyrics and away
from life's pain.

Refurbished Dreams

Refurbished dreams awaken me,
Beckon me as light emerges in the darkness.
A new hope arises.
I am filled with a sense of warmth.
Reserves of strength I did not know I possessed build within me.
No longer paralyzed by my insecurities, I stand tall,
Allow myself to think about the future.
I open my eyes to new opportunities.
Dreams so long ago forgotten are no longer hushed.
As I look around I smile.
The darkness that haunted my life has faded.
A rainbow arches in front of me.
I give myself permission to be who I am
And take the risks I have longed to take.
Dreams are now within my reach.

THE REDWOOD COAST

Memories of another time flood my mind;
A time when I felt peace and enjoyed much of life.
So often I long to return to that oasis among the redwood trees.
The cool air blowing in from the ocean; the scent of redwood trees summoning me back.
Memories of the time I spent under its magical scent fill me with gratitude.
Sometimes I wish I could return to the Redwood Coast;
Bring back to life the times of a quarter century ago.
I wonder if it would be the same if I returned.
The area has changed, progressed with the passage of time.
The magic of the Redwood Coast, the small-town charm may not be the same.
It is not the same just as I am not the same person.
I have lost the quietude of mind brought out by my time in the redwoods.
Those years are locked forever in my mind.
At times I close my eyes.
I see the giant redwood trees; hear the waves crashing upon the beach.
They are calling me back.
Unfortunately my life has changed.
I know I can never return to the past.
Time changes with us; prevents us from returning to a simpler life.
For now I treasure my memories; know that I cannot run away to the past.
The serenity of the Redwood Coast resides inside of me.
I need only close my eyes to call upon it.
My mind's visits are brief, but long enough to provide a sense of calm.

A Battle of Thoughts

The thoughts assembling within my mind attempt to derail my progress.
Knock me off of the tracks.
Thoughts full of self-ridicule and negativity override my desire to focus on the positive.
Affirming thoughts are new residents in my mind.
They have yet to fully take root,
But these thoughts are ready to battle the powerful cynicism that rules my thoughts.
I must gather my strength; give power to the affirming thoughts.
Let them build their determination to overrun the force of the thoughts that try to keep me down.
The battle rages.
I feel weak; stumble and fall to the ground.
As my knees hit the ground I hear the positive thoughts whispering words of encouragement.
Slowly I stand upon unsure legs.
Wonder if these thoughts can really lift me.
I feel the slaps of negativity battering my mind,
But after each blow, softening words echo.
Gaining confidence from these words I meet the challenge head on;
Form words of my own.
I speak aloud to the negative thoughts.
Let them know their power over me is waning.
Still, negative thoughts strike out at me.
Their blows grow weaker as affirming thoughts strengthen me.
I engage in battle.
Realize for the first time in my life that I can win.
The negative thoughts begin to retreat.
Their grip over me loosens.
A smile emerges on my lips.
I am finally in control of my own mind.

AWAY FROM FEAR

Fear plagues my life;
Stymies my progress.
For so long I have hidden from all life has to offer.
Afraid to let myself grow.
Never allowing myself to take even the smallest risk.
Insecurity is my hallmark.
Fear has reigned for too long.
I must take over my life.
Gain a control I have never possessed.
One fear at a time, I take small steps away from anxiety
Slowly create a distance.
I can no longer allow fear to control me.
With each challenge I overcome, fear takes a back seat to all that is
right in my life.

THE GIFT OF DEPRESSION

The gift of depression unwraps itself,
Allows me to see life through different lenses.
Various perspectives provide me with a unique outlook on life.
I know the pain of loneliness brought on by depression,
Experience apathy in its full force.
Watch human interaction from afar.
See the smiles of others and wonder where mine is hiding.
Despite the lowered mood state, I persevere.
The gift of depression stems from introspection.
I am always thinking.
The thoughts have no turn-off valve that would enable me to pro-
cess words and actions.
Depression paralyzes me, thrusts me into darkness.
So how can it be a gift?
Depression allows me to ride a journey toward the light of healing.
A bumpy journey with many twists and turns.
Depression drags me down, but when I arise
I am a stronger person.

OUT OF THE STRUGGLE

The struggle is real.
I feel it rising inside of me.
Its hold tightens like a vise grip.
As I glance around I search for a safe place; somewhere I can escape.
There is so much around me, but nowhere offers the calm I need.
The struggle intensifies.
My mind questions everything.
Scrutinizes my actions; tears apart my thoughts.
I am in pieces, not literally, but functionally.
The struggle prevents me from achieving my true potential.
It leaves me lying in a pool of self-doubt.
Unable to swim in this pool, I strain to stay afloat.
Daily routines become more difficult.
Stressors overwhelm me.
The battle wears on me.
I try to remain positive, but the negativity in my mind gains strength.
Still I find strength inside of me; harness its power.
Slowly I rise.
The pool of self-doubt gradually drains.
Hope replaces the negativity.
I climb one step at a time until I am above the struggle.
The struggle is still real, but now I am winning the battle.

JOURNEYS

My journey begins anew.
I have traveled from darkness into light and back again.
Now new hues await me.
Vibrant colors infuse my journey.
Shadows hide in the recesses.
My expedition through life continues.
Shades of dark and light still fix their grasp upon me from time to time,
But these shades are renewed with seldom–before–seen colors.
My journey is invigorated with fresh energy.
Instead of dark gray clouds and rain, the brilliant arch of a rainbow welcomes me.
A sense of peace settles upon me.
My steps become less hesitant.
I become more confident.
This journey takes me to new places, colorful places.
The bright orange glow of the sun guides me;
Lights the path I am following and
Allows me to enjoy this journey.

Quieting Anxiety

Anxiety festers inside of me.
I feel the heat building,
Like magma bubbling within a volcano.
Taking a deep breath, I attempt to calm the anxiety.
Just like a volcano rumbles I feel a rumbling within my chest.
I take a step back;
Remind myself that anxiety is just false anticipation of what may not happen.
If I distract myself I can prevent the anxiety from erupting.
For me distraction comes in the form of rock music.
I turn to my favorite band, Styx.
They never fail me.
Turning up the volume I allow the music to fill me.
The lyrics take over my thoughts.
The band is always willing; always there for me.
As I listen, the songs soothe the rumbling volcano of anxiety.
The rumbling slows; my chest pain eases.
I regain focus and see the situation from a new perspective.
The festering anxiety has quieted.

CHANGES IN MOOD

Heartened by recent changes in my mood
I reach out to others; attempt to engage in life.
This has never been easy for me.
A lifetime of self-rejection has left me socially inept.
I am mindful of my difficulties.
Yet I know I must put forth the effort;
Place myself in uncomfortable situations.
The benefits outweigh the risks even if they are difficult to fathom.
My mood has improved.
The constant negativity has eased its grip upon me.
I can see the positives in my life.
Realizing I do not have to be alone, I allow myself to interact.
At first I feel naked and stared at,
But I am not rejected.
Gaining confidence, I continue to reach out.
Slowly I let my defenses down.
I am no longer hiding in the background of life.
Stepping into life I am renewed.
Hope begins to trickle into my mindset.
I realize I have something to offer the world.
Others accept me for who I am.
No longer clamped down by my mood, I am a part of life.

HUMBOLDT'S EMBRACE

On a flight bound for the redwoods I wonder if it will still feel like home.
Many years have passed since I last felt the cool breeze of the Redwood Coast.
Memories fill my mind.
I think back to a much different time in my life.
Times have changed;
So have I.
I remember the lush green of the forest and the crashing of the ocean's waves.
As the plane bumps along I can almost feel the ocean water,
The wet sand clinging to my feet,
And the soft ground beneath the redwood canopy.
Soon the plane will land.
Clear, blue skies await.
I close my eyes, eager to walk into Humboldt's embrace.

THE DIRT PATH

I follow a dirt path into a dark forest.
With each step the pain fades more and more.
A dampness fills the air.
I breathe in its chill.
Baby deer drink water from a clear stream.
In the distance I hear the chirping of birds.
I continue walking.
The giant redwoods surround me.
The path twists and narrows.
Still I follow.
The sun's rays peek through the canopy,
Filling me with warmth.
My mind is at peace, soothed by the forest's gentle aura.

Friends on the Journey

For years I have been on a journey.
It has been a winding road
With hills to climb and
Valleys to emerge from.
Often I have felt like giving up.
The journey seemed too much,
But I have persevered, given all I have.
The journey has made me the person I am.
Times of depression when life seemed at its bleakest
Brought me down;
Forced me to seek the assistance of others.
I realized I could not continue the journey alone.
I needed to open myself up to others,
Friends who would support me without judging.
They are my lifeline, beacons of light on the dark journey.
There are times when I resist, afraid I do not have the strength to
continue.
It is when the hills seem steepest that I need the understanding of
my friends.
It does not take much.
Just knowing I am not alone helps.
Life's journey is not meant to be traveled alone.
As I have learned to accept help,
My journey has become easier to travel.

THE LIGHT'S WARMTH

Light peeks through the darkness.
Lifts me up, eases my pain.
Embraced in the warmth of the light, I take new strides.
I move toward my goals,
Open up to the world.
I welcome the light.
Allow its presence to strengthen me.
With each step I take the light becomes brighter.
I see more clearly.
The path ahead of me widens.
New opportunities are within my grasp.

MENTAL STRENGTH

Mental strength used to be foreign to me;
A trait I longed for, but did not possess.
Now I am building that strength one day at a time.
It is not always easy.
I am in training and need reminders from time to time.
My mind is stronger than it used to be.
I can now say no when I mean no;
Say yes only when I want to.
Expressing myself is a little easier.
It is within my mind's power to let others know how I feel.
I still have strength to gain, lessons to learn.
My mental strength is developing.
I am becoming the person I was meant to be.

Garden of Life

A blade of grass, a rose petal
Each insignificant on their own.

Blades of grass, rose petals
Together create a beautiful garden.

A green lawn edged by red rose bushes
I sit on the grass, sniff the rose's fragrance and
Soak in the sunlight.

Remember that I, too, am a part of a garden.
While lost in insignificance on my own,
With others by my side the beauty of life shines.

LIFE IS A GARDEN

Life is a garden.
Flowers bloom, birds sing.
A butterfly lands on a blossom.
We must tend our garden; pull the weeds when they take root.
The sun will rise and set.
Our garden will continue to grow.
Thrive if we allow it.

Life is a garden.
White orchids tinged with purple attract a bumblebee.
We must water our garden; sow seeds of love.
A gentle breeze scatters pollen.
The garden's colors mingle.
Thrive if we allow it.

Life is a garden.
Vibrant roses glisten with the morning dew.
The scents of jasmine and lavender fill the air.
We must pause; breathe in the beauty that surrounds us.
The day will merge into night then rise again.
The garden will awaken with the morning sun.
Thrive if we allow it.

Life is a garden.
Painted with peonies and marigolds.
Nature's hues impressed upon us
Provide the backdrop of our lives.
As our lives imitate the garden,
We pass through the seasons;
Thrive with the inner beauty shared by the garden.

Whale Journeys

Gazing back over turbulent waters I see my life reflected in the waves.
Ups and downs, crashes and lulls.
My journey is carried within the tide.
The salty water pulls me under.
My gaze falls upon a majestic humpback whale.
Gliding right beside me, the whale returns my gaze.
I sense a connection as if the whale understands me.
The whale swims beneath me;
Gently lifts me to the surface.
I breathe for a moment.
Just as gently we go back under the water;
Swim farther out to sea.
I am at ease.
My companion protects me from the darkness of the ocean's depths.
The whale's song lulls me into a sense of calm.
We continue swimming as if we are one.
The whale breaches; breaking through the ocean's surface.
As I hold on I feel exhilarated.
We flip back beneath the surface.
The sun shines above us.
The water glistens.
We swim, my humpback friend and I.
The turbulent waters have calmed.
As I gaze forward I see a peaceful horizon reflected in the vast ocean.

THE DARKNESS FADES

There is a light emanating from deep within the tunnel.
I see it flickering in the distance; use it as my guide.
The source of the light is unclear.
Even though I have taken many steps, the light's distance remains constant.
Still I continue forward.
I am drawn toward the light;
Recognize its warmth.
As I reach for it my fingers fall just short.
I stretch myself; continue reaching for the light.
The walls of the tunnel seem to widen.
Slowly I inch closer.
Soon I realize my hand has emerged from the tunnel into the light.
I feel the warmth;
Take in the glow as it radiates around me.
The light provides an unfamiliar security.
I continue forward with a newfound strength.
The darkness fades behind me.
Finally, I am immersed in the light.

THE POWER OF WRITING

SAFETY

I hide behind my poetry,
Safe within the recesses it creates.
No harm can come to me when my poetry protects me.
Words become my shield.
A pen, my sword.
The fear I harbor in my mind becomes the ink upon lined paper.
Poetry is all I have.
It has become all I need to survive.
Poems protect me from the pain.
Poetry allows me to shun human contact;
Shield myself from human interaction.
My poetry heals me as it isolates me within its recesses.

ALIVE

My poetry connects me to life;
Provides a safety net when I stumble.
Scribbled words fill the page.
Words escape the prison of my mind.
A sense of calm slowly permeates my body.
The words continue their flow,
Releasing the jumbled thoughts that wreak havoc within my mind.
As the words flow I become stronger, more whole.
I am able to reach out to others.
No longer alone, I connect to people who care.
My life changes, I change.
I am finally alive.

RELIEF FOR MY SOUL

When my mind becomes overwhelmed with senseless chatter
I return to the poetry.
The words cannot remain inside of me.
Within me their toxicity slowly drains my life,
But when the words are released into a poem I find hope.
True healing emerges as the poems form.
Like a salve, poetry provides relief for my soul;
Allowing me to express the emotions that have been stifled within me.
Words flow from open wounds.
The poison that is anxiety drips out leaving a stain on the page.
From time to time the stain fades,
But it always returns.
Like tattoos permanently inked onto my flesh.
Poems remind me that my struggle may not be over,
But the poetry will remain an outlet for the senseless chatter.

INK

Meaningful scribbles of ink scrawled across the page.
Expressing my innermost emotions,
Providing a glimpse of what I feel.
Words formed in ink speak of the depression and anxiety I experience.
Sometimes they flow, other times my pen starts and stops.
Whatever the pace, the words allow me to release the thoughts that taunt me.
My words form poems.
Poems of sadness and despair,
Poems of hope and gratitude.
For so long I was hesitant to share these words.
Now I have opened my journal,
Exposed my words to judgment and ridicule in an attempt to offer hope to others.

THE POWER TO HEAL

A poem has the power to heal.
Words scrawled upon the page release raw emotion;
Allow pain to surface and joy to radiate.
The words may be simple, but their strength is immeasurable.
I write to heal myself and
Hope to pass that healing on to others.
Maybe bring a sense of understanding to someone in need or a smile
to another's face.
Then I will know that poetry has truly healed me.

LETTERS

Courageous words shared with others.
A sense of familiarity, a knowing understanding.
Words creating a common bond.
Announcing there is hope, a light after the darkness.
As I read I become aware that I am not alone.
Others have followed similar paths;
Searched for the same healing, given up hope, and searched again.
A kinship of emotional pain is extended to those who are suffering.
Simple, yet powerful words written for you and me fill the pages.
We relate to each other's experiences, understand each other's struggles.
Letters written from a place of light bring a sense of hope to those lost in the darkness.

Inspired by "The Recovery Letters"

A Poem's Pain

I lost my way as I wrote a poem.
Ink spilled onto the page,
But the words made little sense.
My pen kept moving across the page.
Lines filled with scribbled ink that only I understood.
My innermost thoughts poured out.
I could not control the flow.
The words jumped across the page forming lines incoherent to any-
one else's mind.
I reread the words that have formed the poem,
Found my pain spilled out onto the page.
Closing my journal, I attempted to hide from the world,
Yet it was no use.
The words had been written,
The pain escaped to the surface of my life,
Finally exposed.

POETIC JOURNEY

For me writing poetry is a journey.
A calling from deep within;
Beckoning me to follow the scribbles of ink.
Travel along with the words.
Poetry becomes my passport;
Allowing me to venture beyond the present moment
Into the chasm of my thoughts.
A serenade meets me.
Lyrical thoughts lead the way,
A beacon in the dark.
Poetry transports me, carries me through life.
Poetry, a journey, my journey, calling me to new horizons.

POETIC WORDS FLOW

Poetic words flow.
I am humbled by the words.
Ink upon paper,
Symbols of my deepest thoughts.
Poems speak for me; allow my voice to be heard.

Poetic words flow.
I offer a glimpse inside my mind.
Thoughts translated into words.
Insight from my perspective.
Poems communicate my perceptions; give awareness to my inner
self.

Poetic words flow.
I write words that are difficult to utter in speech.
Words of pain and isolation;
All that I feel.
Poems release the negative; allow me to search for the positive.

Poetic words flow.
I communicate a sense of hope.
Light penetrating the darkness;
Illuminating my reality.
Poems express my desire to heal; give rise to all that I have become.

MY PEN ROLLS ACROSS THE PAGE

I write because I have something to say.
Words inside of me beg to be released.
My pen rolls across the page,
Sharing my thoughts.
I have a message I hope can help others;
Bring healing to someone.
Inspire another.
These words clamor to be written.
As I scrawl words upon the page I give them life.
Infuse my words with potential.
I allow myself to be heard
And others to hear me.

WITHIN ME

The blank page beckons me.
It is asking for a poem,
But I am unusually hesitant.
Unsure of what to write,
My pen hovers above the page.
It is ready to let the blue ink flow,
But I hold back my thoughts.
I stare at the blankness of the page;
Wonder where the words have gone.
There are words inside of me, but today they hide.
The barrel of the pen rotates between my fingers.
Ink burning inside.
Words ready to spill out.
I touch the tip of my pen to the page and begin to write.
I experience a sense of relief.
The words are not lost.
Poems still reside within me.

MY JOURNAL

I have found safety in the pages of my journal.
With a blue pen I scribble words upon its lines;
Form poems portraying my journey.
Simple words join together to express my thoughts.
Releasing these thoughts eases my pain.
Allows me to function and be a part of life.
Poetry is my salve.
Safe within the pages of my journal, I write.

My Day Begins

The orange sun is just beginning to rise.
A gray-blue sky lingers.
The moon is still overhead.
My day starts in a coffee shop as I put pen to paper.
I stare out the window hoping for inspiration.
The sky slowly lightens, blue overtaking the gray.
A poem forms on the page.
As I continue to write, I wonder where it will lead me.
Words usher my emotions into the light of a new day.
Each morning I begin with a pen in my hand.
I welcome this time to write;
Realize its effect on me.
So each day I carve out this time;
Make it a part of my routine.
Writing centers me
As my pen leads me into the day.

An Open Journal

I sit with an open journal in front of me.
My pen is poised to write, unleash the thoughts held within my mind.
As I start to write, I hesitate,
Unsure of where the thoughts will lead me.
Soon I am lost within a poem.
Ink streams across the page.
Words flow as the poem takes shape.
My pen does not rest.
I write and write.
Poetry has become my voice.
When I cannot speak I turn to the pages of my journal.
The poems I write replace my speaking voice;
Communicate to others what I cannot say.
Poetry allows me to be heard.
The more I write, the stronger I become.
As each poem is completed I am more whole.
With an open journal I am free to be me.

THE POWER OF MY PEN

I write poems to soothe the pain.
Penned words express my emotions.
My pen becomes my sword,
Defending me, keeping me safe.
I let the words flow as they choose.
I write what I feel;
Allow the words to fill the page.
Soon a poem takes shape.
Simple words merge together to convey my emotions.
Poems reveal who I am, what I have experienced.
My journey through darkness expressed in a poem.
Words joined together provide me with healing;
Bring light into my world.
On the surface they are mere poems.
Below the surface lies a curative power;
A power that soothes my pain and allows me to be whole.

Hidden Behind My Pen

When the struggle becomes too dark,
I hide behind my pen.
Writing line after line of verse,
I allow the words to ease the pain.
Ink flows, carrying the emotions that have been bottled up inside of me.
Secure within the pages of my journal, my thoughts and feelings loosen their grip on me.
The pages fill with word after word.
Poems utter what I cannot say aloud.
I sense the darkness of my struggle lighten,
Feel calmness settle upon me.
As I write, a light appears in the darkness.
I relax, even if only for a brief time.

OUR WORDS

Have we ever stopped to listen to our words?
Really heard what we have said to one another?
A mere sentence, a single word, holds so much power.
Yet often we do not realize the capacity of our own words.
We merely speak without forethought.
Unintentionally hurting the ones we speak to,
But we are so busy we never give our words a second thought.
However, our listeners do.
The mere sentence, the single word repeats over and over in their minds.
The damage is done. The pain cannot be erased.
Three words can begin the healing if we have the courage to say them.
"I am sorry."
A powerful sentence that can mend the wound.
We must think of others before we speak;
Understand the power of our words.

THE POTENCY OF A SINGLE WORD

The power of a single word can bring a smile or deflate a soul.
A single word has potency.
Words are gifts allowing us to communicate.
We can share a feeling.
We can let another know how much we care.
But if we are not careful our words can express unintended meaning;
Hurt those we have no intention of hurting.
A single word contains more power than we realize.
When spoken hastily a word can cause pain without you even realizing what you said.
A single word has the same ability as a bullet;
Can be used like a sword to deftly pierce a soul.
Choose your words carefully.
Realize what you are saying.
You may never know the effect of a mere spoken word.

CPSIA information can be obtained
at www.ICGtesting.com
Printed in the USA
FSHW020507300421
80992FS